A QUARTER OF AN HOUR

Leanne O'Sullivan was born in 1983, and comes from the Beara peninsula in West Cork. She received an MA in English in 2006 from University College, Cork, where she now teaches. The winner of several of Ireland's poetry competitions in her early 20s (including the Seacat, Davoren Hanna and RTE Rattlebag Poetry Slam), she has published four collections, all from Bloodaxe: *Waiting for My Clothes* (2004); *Cailleach: The Hag of Beara* (2009), winner of the Rooney Prize for Irish Literature in 2010; *The Mining Road* (2013); and *A Quarter of an Hour* (2018).

She was given the Ireland Chair of Poetry Bursary Award in 2009 and the Lawrence O'Shaughnessy Award for Irish Poetry in 2011, and received a UCC Alumni Award in 2012.

LEANNE O'SULLIVAN

A Quarter of an Hour

BLOODAXE BOOKS

ISBN: 978 1 78037 222 8

First published 2018 by
Bloodaxe Books Ltd,
Eastburn,
South Park,
Hexham,
Northumberland NE46 1BS.

www.bloodaxebooks.com
For further information about Bloodaxe titles
please visit our website or write to
the above address for a catalogue.

Supported using public funding by
**ARTS COUNCIL
ENGLAND**

Cover design: Neil Astley & Pamela Robertson-Pearce.

Printed in Great Britain by Bell & Bain Limited, Glasgow, Scotland, on
acid-free paper sourced from mills with FSC chain of custody certification.

for Éamonn Ó Carragáin

In wildness is the preservation of the world
THOREAU, *Walden*

ACKNOWLEDGEMENTS

Acknowledgements are due to the editors of the following publications in which some of these poems first appeared: *Cherish, Cherish, Cherish: Reflections on the 1916 Proclamation* (Collins Press, 2016), *Connotation Press, Fermata: Writings inspired by Music* (Artisan House Editions, 2016), *The Irish Examiner, The Irish Times, Lines of Vision: Irish Writers on Art* (Thames and Hudson, 2014), *New Eyes on The Great Book* (Southword Editions, 2014), *Poetry, The Quarryman* and *The SHOp.*

My thanks are also due to Patrick Cotter at the Munster Literature Centre, the School of English at University College, Cork, and The Arts Council of Ireland / An Chomhairle Ealaíon.

I would like to express my deepest gratitude to the staff of Cork University Hospital and the National Rehabilitation Hospital for their tireless support and care, and as always to our family and friends.

Finally, I would like to thank my husband, Andrew King, the closest reader of these poems, for giving me permission to publish them and, especially, to include in this collection the sequence 'The Garden' written in the voice of the hero.

CONTENTS

III

When I was a fox
I could see the fires
spreading across the valley
and I set out to find him.

I

The Cailleach to the Hero

'Stranger, I can tell you no new thing.
The way into darkness is open –

all day and all night old Donn holds watch
on the deep Atlantic where the dead assemble,
on an island rock hewn to a cavern
that's open end to end and shines like gold
when sunlight passes through. There the birds

flying in over the rock bring him sweat meal
and the whole island is bathed in that essence.
When the light of the setting sun pierces
the cave and is cast along the water
then the road between the living and the dead

lies open, until the sun falls again below
the earth and disappears. And this is night,
though it has a darkness that is slight
and a twilight glimmering from the west.
You will see, the way down is easy –

lowlands of the earth and man's deepest self,
the poisons, the waste and debris of this world
you will meet without difficulty, and
although you will be alive you will be dead,
you will have the look of death like the others,

for all those others who have spoken for you here.
But if you decide to retrace your steps,
to bring yourself back to the world you came from
do it quickly, and leave nothing behind.
It is never enough to return as a mere shadow

in the flame, a likeness longing to speak.
But to return, to feel your whole self kicking
and gasping, to cry out loud and clear from
the shoreline, body and soul intact, believe me,
that is the real labour, that will be your work.'

The Fox

We were just returning home
       when the light began to fade,
              that gold
quiet brilliance you waited for at the gate,
       when we crossed the lane
for the last time and suddenly came

to the open-mouthed body of the fox
       lying on the road ahead of us,
her tail flared out behind her, her fur
all live and glandular in the evening air.

              The day
was still warm along her shoulders
       and in the one exploded eye
that held a shape you could not recognise,
the name of the river folding back along
the river, the bright trails, the way
             to the long grasses
and whatever had passed
through there in the night.

And before it all vanished into darkness
you had lifted her
into your arms, and gestured to me,
            and gently
set her down like a small fire
       among the grasses,
so soft, you said she could almost pass
through you in that light.

And what happened next?
        Did the great pain come?

You forget. When we came back
the next morning she was gone.

No sign or scent, no brightness
in the trails, no memory bearing down.

But mine to tell now
                with all the clearness
of the morning after.

      You see,
by the time sunlight had passed through
        the last amber and orbit
of her eye we had just been setting out.
She had already
             become part of this story.

Lightning

No wind, no rain, but every bolt that staggered
from the cumulus that night seemed to raise
a frenzy in the hemispheres of his brain.

I held my husband's head in the damp nest
of my palms, watched the tremors in his eyes
turn and turn like tiny whirlwinds, until

all that I loved was lost in lightning, darkness,
fire. And when the anaesthetic began
to ferry him down a calmer circle,

to wait out the night, I praised his strength,
the goodness of his body – every working cell
and keeper of his passage I prayed defend him,

I let him go. Near midnight the nurse shone
her torch over the still lakes of his eyes,
and I thought of sleeping Odysseus safe beneath

his quilt of leaves, his face smooth like wax-paper,
no piercing rain, no drenched gales or beating heat
upon him. No movement, she said. No light.

The Watchman

...and now I watch for the light, for the signal fire

AGAMEMNON, tr. Robert Fagles

Oh Lord, grant me tonight my clearest sight
and compass my watch with a steady eye
for fear I dream I'm swept away this time.

I saw the bright millstone lower again to the sea
and the stars telling our fortunes in a gaining wind –
friends who've fallen on the way, ambition, envy,

too much dreaming. How shall I keep staying?
In the middle of the longest night I woke trembling
on the staff of my elbows but recognised enough

to make my living real: a foothold in the earth,
my grove against the currents and those cold,
Martello fires, our great, silent heralds of the sky.

Nothing happened but the dark, the skin
of the dark repeating,
                              Shake yourself, Sentry.
Look alive.

Autumn

How the autumn dawn burned through
the misty broods and settled down in fire;

how quickly the sun glittered my shadow,
how my shadow cried, a moment, with joy.

A light frost, a vision of light crackling
down the maples, down the tinder ash.

I was the good thief. I held my love's
sweet breath, his beautiful, intelligent gaze.

I closed my eyes and he woke inside me.
When I saw, he saw the inflamed world.

A bird sang deeply from the gutter eaves.
When I closed my eyes I was elsewhere.

I walked through the fire of his sleep.

Tracheotomy

I waited outside your room and imagined
the incision's deep crimson pool
in the hollow love-notch of your throat.

So silent and unbreathing as to be almost
gone from me. What were the last words
you spoke? Tell me about love,

curling up among the vocal reeds,
filmy-white, beams on a footbridge, fascia,
muscle, isthmus, your domain of secrets,

of rained-on tributaries, rooted and grafted
onto the machines, when I came in,
and I could see the wound pulled wide

by the cannula, its dark, weeping undulations.
I felt like the woman who gazed and gazed into
the mouth of the little god. I saw everything.

A Nativity

Of course things had gone from bad to worse,
with the storm outside near washing the world away
and everyone flocking to the chapel for shelter.

How strange, then, drawing closer to the scene –
the empty crib, the petrified Magi – to find him there,
the one clay Rabbit at the centre of it all,

as though a god of the spring-time had mysteriously
risen or rolled a stone back from our minds.
His outstretched paws, his round, dark eyes

in one sense made him human; whose gaze
was gentleness, a thief who was friend to many,
or a beggar whose beauty shone in his seeing you.

He remembered the darkness of the true forest,
understood the fall of light among the trees,
the sound and sleep of absolute sanctuary.

And, no, we did not think to question.
Desperation, he knew, became our defence,
the one cherished seed that was our hope.

Mothers and fathers who had not knelt in years
bowed before him and murmured in harmony,
so that a kind of music trickled along the pews,

and was carried on into the night.
For always, they say, there is a light in the storm,
a voice heard in the great essential winds.

And always, it seems, an hour of peace, even
with the world outside trying frantically to come
to an end, and the holy family still a good way off.

The Kitchen Maid

(after 'Kitchen Maid with the Supper at Emmaus' by Velázquez)

All the ceremonies of the kitchen
come through – sunlight on the bread boards
and flour swept up from the bare floors;
so her footsteps vanish like pools of rain

on the road, her swiftness towards the fire
unproven where she heaps the deepest red
around the bastible, enough for
mystery to keep and the soft notes of bread

to rise, companionable, from their dark centre.
The meal table set and laid, the vessels
shining with room for the guest portion,
a sign that means kind labour

without any words or remembrance,
but heard about afterwards, in her absence –
how a certain light breaking across the table
might suddenly set a whole world in motion.

Lord

Now I am told to pray
to the baby Jesus
to take the ailing
soul of my husband away,

but even that miracle
will not stop crying.
4 a.m. alone with the child
howling and refusing

my awkward affections
and stories, dear Lord,
about other redeemable
forms of love.

Prayer

The eyelash that drifted down the broad plane
of your cheekbone comforts me. Is it the archer
travelling across the night sky of your un-
consciousness, his singing bow? Is it an anchor

let down at the spirit doors, the glimmer
of an almost wakening eye? Do you see
through it an aperture of heaven, or a vast sea
that might keep your light-headed stare

fastened and ready? I stoop to draw
it to the tip of my finger, one brief
moment, holding my breath to first allow
your heart monitor its three-note song –

I wish you happiness and long life,
my husband who's been gone from me so long.

Leaving Early

My Love,

       tonight Fionnuala is your nurse.
You'll hear her voice sing-song around the ward
lifting a wing at the shore of your darkness.
I heard that, in another life, she too journeyed
through a storm, a kind of curse, with the ocean
rising darkly around her, fierce with cold,
and no resting place, only the frozen
rocks that tore her feet, the light on her shoulders.

And no cure there but to wait it out.
If, while I'm gone, your fever comes down –
if the small, salt-laden shapes of her song
appear to you as a first glimmer of earth-light,
follow the sweet, hopeful voice of that landing.
She will keep you safe beneath her wing.

The Cailleach to the Widow

(after Lucille Clifton)

Fair? Don't talk to me about fair.
When I came to the river in spate
I could only carry one of my two
companions across it with me,
tucking him safely under my arm,
leaving the other trembling behind us
in the dark, casting his profanities.

Now let those things stay unreconciled.
How they bewitch you into thinking
everything can be saved.
But that is not what you want.
You want to save only what you love,
which is a form of suffering,
immaculate, leaving no scar.

And you know this already,
as you hold your arms out toward
the other shore, still determined
to make any bargain, to grasp what's
left of the world you came from,
the light failing fast, the waters
rising quickly around you.

Oracle

Now, an old truth rises to its zenith
in my adult life, a tide at sunset suddenly
filling the glooming light. Or perhaps
I hear the midnight prowl of my father's
mother swaying through my head,
repeating news of sickness or of death;

how she'd take *The Book of the Ancestors*
under the soft pelt of her elbow,
ascend the landing in her nightdress
and disappear with a labouring fullness
into the moth-pink light of her bedroom,
rooting out relations, uttering her own

continual augury, her common-sense portent.
So trancelike, so quietly pronounced, I almost
didn't believe when she herself was gone,
and we sat around her chair that morning after,
until someone said it, finally – *tiocfaidh ár lá*,
my glimmerwoman of the small hours.

The Lark Ascending

(after 'The Lark Ascending' by Ralph Vaughan Williams)

The moment the lark finally vanishes
into the spread green sky of the forest
is the moment you suddenly lift

your bruised arm up, over your body,
as though to show me the wing's eclipse,
or the wing, or the season of your dream.

And even as your hand lapses silent
onto your chest, and your breath goes
sluggish, I am already watching your feet

prepare their slow first step under the sheet
as the last notes of sunlight fall quiet,
and you do not move again. Oh, my dreamer,

are you a bird reviving in a summer field?
Was it the lark ascending that you heard,
a ghost among its shy-hearted tunes?

Yes. I heard the lark escaping, too.

Waking

(in memory of William King)

Your father, in fact, in his flying days,
having ascended so far into thin air
and for just a moment hovering there,
like that unfallen, untoppled charioteer,
out on his own and making waves,
buoyed and giddy and bound by the very space

he was gazing into. And long enough
to have known the weight of that atmosphere
shudder in his bones, to see starlight
true and unbending, the horns of Taurus,
the Archer's steady bow, the dream behind
the dream and no one, and nothing else.

And how it was closer than he could
have ever believed. Still, they said,
his real gift was knowing the exact moment
to bring it all to life again. So watch him now
where he banks the plane across pure limbo,
firing and igniting for all he's worth,

a bearing down toward nothing but solid earth
where the air thickens and thunders around him,
and that final rupture, like the needle's eye
being split, a clearing boom that's sent
the animals scattered and galloping on the farms
below, and your father, hearing nothing of it.

His Vision

As he woke up Andrew began to talk
as a way of knowing himself again
talking and talking about his journey
about the wild animals he saw
and the birds of time he said their voices
wakened back to him a certain knowledge
what he should become and how to return
a way he could not really touch with words
the stare of the fox vanished beside him
the serpent's aim the flare of the swallow
always passing just beyond his reach
but he kept on speaking anyway trying
to understand something of their call
even in his soundest sleep it was one word
then another word until their shadows
the gold glowing coins of their eyes
had lit up the burned out paths around him
throwing their light back across the trail
to see that he was still following
he said he could always see them
those first days and nights I remember
I would lie down next to him and watch
the bare animal shapes of his mouth
as they came to pass broken and guttural
sometimes calling over the great mountains
sometimes stopping in the dark to wait for him
he said he could always hear them just
breathing beneath the sound of his breathing

II

The Cailleach to The Widow

Hazel

could have been

my first word

delivering in its carriage

the smell of the new earth

the haul of ravens

in its green court

do not give it meaning

it was nothing

(it is everything)

began the voice in my head

Love, where are we now?....

Love, where are we now? He gazes round
the ward, his small bed-space, working it out.
Bermuda? he asks, smiling at me fondly.

No, try again, I say. *Cuba?* The nurse
comes to start his IV line, and when she goes,
he goes, *somewhere in the South Pacific?*

which sounds all right to me; and anywhere else
he wants I smile along beside him, thinking
how good, how pleasant it is to sit together,

Lethe-drunk like spirits in their second bodies,
come far from the world of vanishing paths –
to know sunlight from the open window

playing on his hands, the tender city breeze,
and all the while adoring the early birdsong
he hears steadily cheeping from the machines.

Eumnestes

When I arrived in this country for the first time
I had in my possession only one book,

and being almost completely alone wrote
in such detail everything I could remember

                                    – the big bang,

the years of Nestor, the great disasters
and disturbances of weather; world ending

and world beginning, blue unto great darkness
unto blue again; unto temples and courtyards,

unto kingdoms and faltering customs.
Not that I fully understood, but in this way

I have been useful, have minded how they lived,
how they harvested, cotton or grain,

what seed caught in the amber drop.

How once a man might have luckily sensed
the danger meant for him, something creeping

in the great, dark expanse, just before he decided
to turn around and come back, find another way.

How he listened, carefully, watched for signs,
for trails, or deciphered how a peal of light

falling through the trees could mark
roughly a way in, the way out again,

so that he knew the path in the future must be –

Which is the reading I try to bear in mind.

Morning Poem

Of course memory began in the garden,
going out to it so early that first morning home,
the little bells of the dawn not yet too loud
or too deep, the world around him still
only half asleep. Oh Byzantium, he thought,

fingering the spires of the foxgloves,
and the berries ghosting along the bramble,
and the beams grown rotten into the ground.
The things we have seen, the sweet,
accidental parts of our lives stooping largely

in their rough matins. *Where are we now?*
Somewhere near him a stone unsettles itself
and a beast in the blue light turns over.
What sound do you make to find that?
What symbol means nothing at all?

When Words

He thought *tree* was *wife*,
returning to the field
with her no longer there.
And for weeks now *field*
was not the same as *home*
when he tried to call out,
so deaf and dumb
that nothing seemed
to answer him or come back.
It was not the tree
he missed, but the sound
for tree, and the fox,
illuminated, as it slipped past.
It was that kind of silence,
the way the earth is vague
before dawn, the first sounds
not yet breaking through.
When does *pond* become *sky*?
he thought, leaning over it,
brain where everything
crawls into detail,
bare and particular
and known completely.
Such a private thing, really,
the world easing out
of nothingness. Remember?
Try it out loud this time,
the pond turning bluish first
then grey. Re-member like that.
It's never as lost as you think.

The Garden

The Pond

'I saw. Then I didn't see.
So what was the word
waiting just below the surface?

Gauzy under leaf-light,
avowed in the muck
and the broken motions
of an earlier sound.

How much easier to have
leaned in, chanced it
flickering out of reach.

To press my ear there,
or follow it to where
it swept so hurriedly
down, out of sight.

To disappear like the night
burning its stars before
trailing off. But how far?

And how long?
Now it becomes a question,
hook-bite on my tongue.
Little creatur-ish. Little pilot.'

Dawn

'*Dawn* is of childhood there, sleeping on the porch
wanting a little less shade, little out of the dream.
Where the light coming in across the sky
was not a place of edges, not a flag rolled out,
but a whole roomful beginning to talk at once.
Softly. And tributaries. And seconds on their deltas
palely stirring, such slow moving that would
keep me tongue-tied and unblinking on the deck,

watching for the swatches of still dark where nothing
had been reached, nothing had happened yet.
Slowly. Until it trills forward to catch up,
tilts the world a little to the right, to the left.
Then the moon, releasing its drowned body
back into the dark. That moment, once it comes,
that here to not here. A quarter of an hour.
A whole quarter of an hour, then it was gone.'

Byzantium...

'Byzantium,' he said, 'this is no coincidence.
That in a wild morning not even broken
I would go out into the world and see you again,
your palaces, your great empire. But not
as I remember it: the old ground exposed
and scorched, the decorated arches and pillars
sunk now into dolmens, lichened and twisting.

And in the heavy, dark waters of the pond,
it's you, Justinian, raised from that anatomy,
both alive and dead and taut with hunger.
Your face looks as though it is dreaming
and in it I see one smouldering man
at the centre of the fabled city. Alone
and completely astonished. Pain beyond pain,

and the whole world burning as he reaches
out to touch it – what seemed so much like love
or daylight, as light appears in dreams,
a single note, or a flare glimpsed along the edge
before it rises, slowly, over the waves of laurel,
over the blossoms and our blackening roots
and the grand spires of our industrial age.'

Fox

'Is the fox you see on your evening walk
by the river the same one who sits
beside me in the garden when I cannot sleep,
gazing out from under the bare limbs
of the orchard, among the brambles
and our tribe of ferns? So, I have come
to a time in my life when I cannot name
one season from another, or remember
what the day means to tell me when the sun
disappears so early out of the world.
I know I am living in the months before
I was born, when the maples would burn
along the twilight and the animals
had all slipped through the last long
shadows of the year. It is just like that
when I try to call out and the words
I had known forever and by heart
drift silently away down the dark lawn.
They have vanished and nothing is heard.
What I want to say is that the fox is here.
She has come so near that I cannot believe it,
her fur all starlit and glittering, warmer
than my own skin against the frost.
Then not a fox, but a woman where she once
had been, sitting beside me on the grass,
speaking gently and with a woman's voice.
My sweetheart, she whispers into the night,
it's time to go back to sleep now.'

Labhraidh Loingseach

(St Patrick's Cathedral, Armagh)

To chance upon him – your first confessor
for so many years, low to the ground,
his bare-breasted stare all eyes and ears,
and himself confessing without a sound;

to admit him from within, then look again
to the wing-span of his arms, the subtle
pounding of his temples that seems to turn
and burn through what he would conceal –

drawing out his animal ears, that animal life.
He stirs a syllable in the air
like an old willow whose song might hook you,
or cast your features in such relief.

Now you see that nothing else can happen:
this body, this weight breaks kindly open.

Mes Aynak

(for Qadir Temori)

'and now I also pray for Mes Aynak'

Out there on the blurred lines of the earth
you are trying to write faster than the light
is fading. Soon the sun will darken

like a thumb-print down the parched walls,
pressing everything gently into sleep.
Are you ready to go now? The shadows

that constellate on the page are endless.
Mountains and sky, sherds and coins
and amphorae, are never enough to tell

how all things pass away, how something
was here to begin with. Is it time to go?
The dark slips in through a net of star-shine

and settles each blown and shattered reliquary,
unseeable, untranslatable, until you turn
to leave it – which is the point, after all:

that original hour of remembering
your place at the gates of the great city
and in light of such remembering, forget.

Dream

A door that opened once onto a great hall
creaks and moans like drift on the ocean floor.
You hear it clearly when you take your place

with the other graduands, and the faint sound
of your own footsteps weaving among them.
You are still dressed in your old gown, restless

and watchful for the porter who will meet you
halfway through. Spirit of doorways, of key-chains
who, in another life, would have tapered his gaze

to chide or look askance when you passed by,
brooding and changeable and earthen in his lodge.
You would hardly know him now, mysterious

and spectral at the edge of the crowd where
he waves you gently over and fastens the new gown
tightly across your chest, its weight and colour

rivalling all the bright world you have known before.
How wonderful, he says, smiling as he touches
your shoulder, before he turns and points the way.

Ghost

I saw then.

     In your sickness I had become
my own ghost, half sensed in the light
that draped beneath the curtains;

     obliterated softly on the landing
when you passed by.

Every shade pulled down. The garden
boarded up, the particular and the waste.

Still, the water glass on the table filling itself,
     over and over.
Plates and cups cleared away.

The little book by your bedside
thumbed through at night, while you slept,
the pages rustling, making sounds like

     'oh the green fields'
and 'the stars light up'
     and 'the world is out there'.

A city, a wilderness,
my own voice reaching out to touch you,
     until
the path of narration suddenly goes dark
     and you cannot hear me.
Not possible
to haul you all the way back, into the light.

But I would.

Having lived once, didn't it seem so ordinary,
that walking safely out into the world?

You knew it even then –
in all of our marvellous existences
no one could have loved you more,
no one would have given as much as I did.

Listen now again:

> Come to the window.
> Draw back the blinds.

> Remember me.

Mountains and sky.
Cinnamon, laughter, dew-light.

> This is what I came back to tell you.

David Copperfield

(for Claire Connolly)

No. No finer thing than to walk through town
with the key of my house in my pocket,
to stop to talk with women and men
of all the easeful talk of cures and debts.

And all the while to know its nickel backed,
winter light turning warm in my hand,
the strike of the bolt-stump, my footing exact
as though I could dream-walk myself back to stand

in the dark of the inner door –
no answer save my own – then gently
lever its weight toward the bright rooms. Oh, hoard
of the free life! Of the sunlit, scattering plenty.

Meteor Shower

If we were looking for cliché, well,
here it is – *the universe is so vast,*
or even better, *isn't it such a small world?*
And smaller still, lying on our backs
on the grass of the back garden
in the most peaceful dark,
the beds tucking up their hems
and the glasshouse hazing over
with its own sleepy breath.

The sky is throwing its one show
across the pelt of the earth,
nimble breezes of light that ricochet
off the atmosphere, that are gone
as soon as they appear.
This one is Eurydice, you say,
already forgetting. This one
Orpheus Perpetual, still terrified
of the truth and trailing after her.

Or the great dragons
of the Orient sweeping through
with their bright, fierce tails.
And there – Li Bo, I think, finally set sail
on a lunar wash, clear of the earth,
and just singing and singing.
Fly me to the moon,
let me live among the stars,
the universal fires that by now

have grown tiny on that horizon,
like gorse smouldering above
the toy-sized villages across the bay.
When I get old, you say, laughing,
I am going out with the mythologies,
Aegospotami, Hsu garden,
one foot in front of the other.
When it's all over,
tell them I did it my way.

And as soon as he starts he stops,
the world having fallen
so flickeringly quiet with watching,
the trees, the grasses even, holding
their breath; the children across the way
swaying in their swings
and still staring up, trying to catch
each absconding flash
before it passes, and half-dreaming –

Perseus vanquishing
the monsters under their beds,
the eye of God, his chariots bravely
drawn by their brother's
wooden horses – and farther on, perhaps,
when the great winds come,
their own cherry blossoms blushing
in the gardens of Jupiter. Those long,
carefree evenings on Mars.

Thunder

It is the animals beginning to return
over the soft belly of the earth.

They have walked a long time
under the same sky with no country,

the dark stream of their bodies rising
into the wind. And they remember

exactly the way, their long shadows
stretching now into the fields,

into the rivers while we watch all day
from our windows, what we thought

was weather or the world in her fever
shaking up on the cleared hill,

a certain thunder gathering underfoot.
Do you not hear it yet?

Look at that man listening.
Something in him is waking up.

Oisín

He hesitates before taking Niamh's hand.
The water is glittering. His horse
is ready, restless in the morning light.
He stands on the wide, white shore,
looking back at the home-place
for the last time. He knows the story
will change in him as time passes,
no matter how well he has learned it,
no matter how well he was taught.
Love and grief. Weeping and singing.
Believing there was magic in the stones.
Mountains and rites and sovereignty.
Always with loss to come, and growing
tired among the heather and vetch.
Still, he thinks, what times we saw,
what astonishment! He keeps trying
to taste that wholeness but cannot.
No matter, he says, looking out towards
the ocean. It is almost spring again.
Tomorrow I will be living on the island,
laughter and birdsong clear from the shore,
sunlight giving way to coolness at night.
I will have fine things, he says, and perfect skies.

Anamnestes

Old Man,
                I am thinking about you today.
The years have taken off, and if you're living only
in my mind and nowhere else I can't be certain.
But in light of everything that has come and gone
I thought it right to make this brief connection.
You see, there was always more to it than just a boy
in the outback of a library, living and growing
among the oakwood stacks, fetching books and histories
when people would knock on your door enquiring –
who they truly were and where they were really from.
Then one late night while you were sleeping,
out of curiosity I crept back in. The lamps were dim
and dampness sweated down the rough stone walls,
but still I gathered and balanced in my arms
all that I could and sat cross-legged upon the floor,
vague as a ghost-boy washed clean of memory,
and began to read: of the history of the courts,
of tribunals and their theatres; of common wealth,
of policies and of law, the sciences and all philosophies.
Then cities of stone and steel were raised up before me –
the grand romancers, the men of the court,
the King's men and the man of solitude,
the man of wisdom and the blind man holding forth,
the man of letters and the man of the world.
Some had their names in books and some in long
parchment scrolls, worm-eaten and canker-holed.
Then in *The Book of the Ancestors* I read them first –
the creatures of the forest and names I had not heard,
before or since, their syllables a blood-knot,
a tonnage in the sound of the sea, in the eye of God,

in the scriptural, ashen geographies; in the moment
of conception, the moment of birth, of love,
of light treading the air, of what's immeasurable,
of the matter of just memory in the rhymes and furies
of all the world – a world I saw I could live in
and in it become anyone. When morning glanced
along the shutters I rose light-headed for the first time
and for the first time in my life I was gone,
travelling down the narrow road with the grass-banks
so heavy-white with snow it felt as though my own
shoulders were broadening out to touch them.
And so the years have passed and it was no easy thing.
You yourself knew that: metaphors of light and always
an image of the road on which we set out.
But now I hope it has not been too long. Eumnestes,
out of the words you wrote mine were borrowed
but followed their own meandering course.
If you are there to read them be sure and know that life
is still turning, and it's a mystery what can be borne.
I say this truthfully because, in the end, I had done it alone –
stood at the step of my own front door, as at the portals
of your house, and breathed the full of it.
I put my ear to the machinery of the deep earth
and listened. I came to understand it myself.

Fox

Halfway along the way a fox appeared
out of the perishing hedgerows and stopped
on the road in front of him,

the lines of her breast straight and clear,
fear having fallen away from there.
What is she doing? He thought. She said,

I am waiting to see what you will do next.
That's funny, he said, beginning to follow,
I am doing the very same thing.

And that was the way they went, morning
after morning, the hedgerows turning
their infinite colours, the body with its one fire.

The Cailleach to the Widow

The Universe said to me,
Old woman I have learned
a few good things,

that when one part dies
in me another comes
tearing through the darkness

like a star, sudden
and tender and painful
as hell. Each time

I have sat at the centre
of the world to see it,
each time I have crawled

the dark of my own belly
to not see, the shape
of the great light coming

and the dying one,
washed in such kindness
rising steadily towards it.

Elegy for the Arctic

Now that we believe in the stories
of your vanishing, you who had
been there all along, outside of time,
you upon whom the light of day
is now burning, our sorrow is such
small economy. Even an hour

sets us apart, is a fragment lost
and drifting through our hands,
like the sun clearing away
the mists above you, and the pools
where you quarry, and the birds
waking close to you in your own music.

We knew you as brightness anchored
in shadow, the body of a perfect
wilderness listening across the tundra.
What do you hear now, as you move out
toward the shore where the whistling terns
pass overhead and into the darkness?

I hope this leaving is as kind to you
as for any elder, any great animal
going the same way. Keep safe
for us the trails that lead back
to level ground, back to the beginning.
I fear those too are disappearing.

Note

If we become separated from each other
this evening try to remember the last time
you saw me, and go back and wait for me there.
I promise I won't be very long,
though I am haunted by the feeling
that I might keep missing you,
with the noise of the city growing too
loud and the day burning out so quickly.
But let's just say it's as good a plan as any.
Just once let's imagine a word for the memory
that lives beyond the body, that circles
and sets all things alight. For I have
singled you out from the whole world,
and I would – even as this darkness
is falling, even when the night comes
where there are no more words, and the day
comes when there is no more light.

III

The Cailleach to the Hero

It's death, isn't it? To grasp and grasp and never let go.
                    Until it comes. That letting go.

But world goes dark then? World slips away?

No, darkness only at first, which was fear.

A moment later, I was awake.

NOTES

The Cailleach to the Hero (12): In Celtic mythology the Cailleach is a sovereignty goddess, a wise woman figure embedded in the physical and mental landscape of the West of Ireland and Scotland. Her petrified remains are located on the Beara Peninsula, Ireland. The lines 'And this is night, / though it has a darkness that is slight / and a twilight glimmering from the west' are from Plutarch's description of Cronus worship in the North Atlantic.

Oracle (27): *The Books of the Ancestors* are a collection of genealogical works about the people and history of the Beara Peninsula, researched and written by Riobard O'Dwyer.

Eumnestes (34): meaning 'good memory', a character who appears in Book II of *The Faerie Queene*, in an allegory of the human body, and occupies one of the three regions of the brain. He is an old man whose task is to be the guardian of memory.

Labhraidh Loingseach (42): according to Irish legend was a High King of Ireland, who had horse's ears, and very long hair to keep them hidden. He had his hair cut once a year and as rule always killed his barbers so that his secret would not be found out.

Mes Aynak (43): meaning 'little source of copper' is an ancient monastic site 40 km south-east of Kabul in Afghanistan. Mes Aynak contains Afghanistan's largest copper deposit and in 2007 was leased to the China Metallurgical Company who intend to destroy the site and everything buried beneath it. Archaeologists have been working to document the site and save as many artefacts as they can. Quadir Temori is one of the Afghan archaeologists featured in the documentary film *Saving Mes Aynak*.

Anamnestes (57): meaning 'able to call to mind / the re-minder', he was an aid to Eumnestes in *The Faerie Queene*, who was too old and feeble to retrieve the books he needed to consult, and so the boy Anamnestes would fetch the books for him.